THE Boo-Boos THAT CHANGED THE WORLD

A TRUE STORY ABOUT AN ACCIDENTAL INVENTION (REALLY!)

Barry Wittenstein • *Illustrated by* Chris Hsu

Charlesbridge

In memory of my mother and father
—B. W.

To Artemis and my entire family,
past and future generations
—C. H.

Text copyright © 2018 by Barry Wittenstein
Illustrations copyright © 2018 by Chris Hsu
All rights reserved, including the right of reproduction in whole or in part in any form.
Charlesbridge and colophon are registered trademarks of Charlesbridge Publishing, Inc.

Published by Charlesbridge
9 Galen Street
Watertown, MA 02472
(617) 926-0329
www.charlesbridge.com

Library of Congress Cataloging-in-Publication Data
Names: Wittenstein, Barry, author. | Hsu, Chris, illustrator.
Title: The boo-boos that changed the world: a true story about an
accidental invention (really!) / Barry Wittenstein; illustrated by Chris Hsu.
Description: Watertown, MA: Charlesbridge, [2018] | Includes webography.
Identifiers: LCCN 2016053955 (print) | LCCN 2017006562 (ebook) | ISBN 9781580897457
    (reinforced for library use) | ISBN 9781632895578 (ebook) | ISBN 9781632895585 (ebook pdf)
Subjects: LCSH: Dickson, Earle, 1892–1961—Juvenile literature. | Johnson & Johnson—
    History—Juvenile literature. | Bandages and bandaging—History—Juvenile literature. |
    Skin—Wounds and injuries—Juvenile literature. | Wounds and injuries—Treatment—
    Juvenile literature. | Medical innovations—History—Juvenile literature.
Classification: LCC RD113 .W58 2018 (print) | LCC RD113 (ebook) | DDC 617.1/3—dc23
LC record available at https://lccn.loc.gov/2016053955

Printed in China
(hc) 10 9 8

Illustrations done in mixed media and Photoshop
Display type set in Pinto No. 03 by Georg Herold-Wildfellner
Text type set in Freekenmacfont by Typotheticals
Color separations by Colourscan Print Co Pte Ltd, Singapore
Printed by 1010 Printing International Limited in Huizhou, Guangdong, China
Production supervision by Brian G. Walker
Designed by Diane M. Earley

ONCE UPON A TIME, in 1917 actually, a cotton buyer named Earle Dickson married his beloved, Josephine, and they lived happily ever after.

THE END.

Actually, that was just the beginning.

The newlyweds expected to live a quiet life in New Brunswick, New Jersey. Instead, Earle and Josephine ended up changing the world, one boo-boo at a time.

You see, Josephine was accident prone. She often bumped and bruised herself while working around the house. But that was nothing compared to how often she injured herself in the kitchen.

OUCH! When she sliced and diced an onion, she sometimes sliced her finger, too.

BOO-HOO! When she grated cheese, she sometimes grated her knuckle.

ARGH! When she lifted a hot pot off the stove, she sometimes burned her hand.

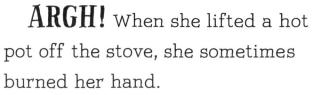

After Josephine winced in pain, she quickly grabbed
a rag to stop the bleeding.

But with bulky towels between her fingers, it was
even harder for Josephine to hold a knife. She became
even more accident prone. Impossible, you say? It's true.
Josephine's klutziness had become a bloody problem!

Every night when Earle came home from work, he looked forward to talking with Josephine and eating the wonderful meal she had prepared. That was until he saw his beloved's hands. Yikes! Her cuts might get infected. He had to help his new bride.

Earle's father was a doctor, so Earle knew a little bit
about boo-boos and bandages. And luckily he worked
for a company that manufactured hospital supplies.
Earle knew there had to be a solution. But what was it?

Earle thought while he shaved in the morning. "Maybe if I . . ."

Earle thought while he bought cotton in the afternoon. "Then I could . . ."

And Earle thought some more while he lay in bed at night. "And that would solve . . ."

Finally a lightbulb went off over his head.
"I'VE GOT IT!" Earle yelled with excitement,
waking up Josephine.

"What have you got?" she asked.

"The bloody solution, of course!" Earle replied.

The next morning Earle tried out his idea.

STEP 1: He took a long piece of adhesive tape and laid it on the kitchen table, sticky side up.

STEP 2: Earle cut small squares of sterile gauze and stuck them on the tape every few inches.

STEP 3: He placed a material called crinoline on top of the adhesive tape to keep the whole strip sterile.

"It's perfect!" Earle said proudly.

Now all Josephine had to do was cut off a piece of the longer strip and put it on. She didn't need anybody's help. She needed only one hand! It worked!

At last, they lived happily ever after.

THE END.

But . . . **WAIT!** Here comes the part about how
Earle and Josephine changed the whole world.

Earle guessed there were probably hundreds, possibly
even thousands, of people who could benefit from his
new invention.

Earle and Josephine thought about making the bandages
themselves. But they soon realized it was too big a job.
Earle told one of his coworkers about it, and the coworker
encouraged Earle to meet with the company's president.

At first Earle's boss, James Johnson, wasn't quite sure Earle's idea was good enough. Earle demonstrated how easy it was to put the bandage on. Then Mr. Johnson saw his own lightbulb. The company agreed to produce and sell the product. They combined the words "bandage" and "first aid" to create the clever name Band-Aid.

Now Earle and Josephine would surely live happily ever after because Band-Aids were guaranteed to be an instant success.

And with that we have come to **THE END.**

Thank you and good night . . .

That first year, Band-Aids were made in a factory. It was a slower-than-slow process, and only a small number could be manufactured by hand. They came rolled up and were eighteen ridiculous inches long and three ridiculous inches wide. And they still had to be cut into pieces. Earle, Josephine, and Mr. Johnson had high expectations, but the Band-Aid boxes collected dust, ignored and unwanted.

A few years later the company invented a machine that could mass-produce thousands of the bandages. Instead of the user having to cut them up, each one was ready to go. Band-Aids were now about three inches long and an inch wide. And they were cute, too. Each one had a little red string to pull in order to open the paper wrapper.

SUCCESS! Band-Aids flew off the shelves.

THE END.

WOODWORKING

ANGLING

BUGLING

PIONEERING

Not really.

Unfortunately, even with the cute red string and the convenient size, the public wasn't sold on the idea. Mr. Johnson knew there had to be a solution. What happened next was truly a stroke of genius.

ARCHERY

ORNITHOLOGY

MASONRY

GEOLOGY

The company decided to give the Band-Aids away. Mr. Johnson wondered who needed self-adhesive bandages the most. And then that lightbulb went off again. The Boy Scouts, of course! All those fall-down, climb-up, scratched-elbows, scraped-knees boys got plenty of cuts. It didn't take long before the mothers of those rough-and-tumble boys saw how handy the little bandages were.

THAT DID IT!

Earle and Josephine's invention was a smash.

During World War II the company sent millions of
free Band-Aids to the brave soldiers fighting overseas.

In the years that followed, Band-Aids were made in
different sizes, colors, and designs. Some even had
pictures of cartoon characters on them.
And that continues to this day, all over the world.

From boisterous hot-dog vendors in Brooklyn, fancy French winemakers, tired taxi drivers in Denmark, and English bobbies on bicycles to daredevil skateboarders in Saskatchewan, king-crab fishermen in Alaska, sweaty Ugandan soccer players, and applauding audiences at the Bolshoi Theatre in Moscow, the sounds of AHIA! WHAA! and OUCH! echo still. But not for long.

ÜFF!

哎唷!

AUA!

痛いっ!

AIE!

AHIA!!

!آخ

Because soon those snivels and sobs of pain are silenced by Earle and Josephine's accidental boo-boo invention. And *that* is the happiest ending of all.

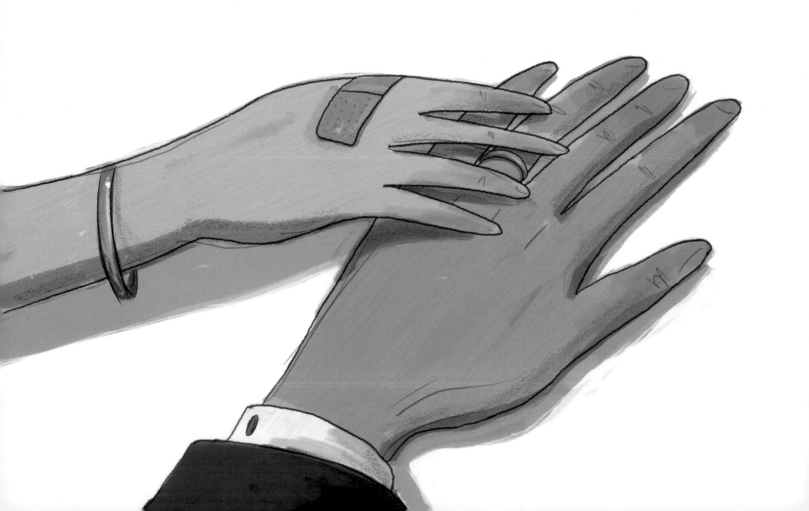

THE END. (Really!)

AUTHOR'S NOTE

We don't know exactly what Earle and Josephine said when Earle first figured out his idea for a ready-made bandage. I invented the dialogue and details surrounding their interactions in this book.

The Band-Aid is one of those little inventions that nobody thinks about much.

You stick one on when you get a boo-boo and continue on your way. What is there to ponder?

There's a whole lot involved. Every invention has a history. Things don't invent themselves, do they? Then who does? And when? And where and how? Inventions are invented because they fill a need.

Such was the case of the Band-Aid. Josephine needed an easy way to stop the bleeding on her fingers and to make sure her cuts didn't get infected. So Earle combined several ideas that resulted in the invention of the Band-Aid, a bandage that anyone could put on by themselves.

It seems like such a simple idea today, but think about all the elements that came together perfectly. Earle's father was a doctor, so Earle was somewhat familiar with the basics of cleaning cuts; Earle happened to work for a major manufacturer of medical supplies; and Earle's wife was accident prone. Take any of those three away, and we can only wonder if the name Earle Dickson would mean anything to anybody in the world.

The world needed small, sterile adhesive bandages, and they would have been invented eventually. Maybe somebody else at Johnson & Johnson would have come up with the idea a few months or years later. Or a competitor might've thought of them first. Maybe even somebody halfway around the world.

Earle was promoted to vice president and was eventually elected to Johnson & Johnson's board of directors. He was certainly rewarded with respect from his colleagues and with a bigger salary, too. That was good news to the Dicksons, who raised two boys.

Earle died in 1961, when he was sixty-eight years old. He didn't see the variety of designs, shapes, and colors that Band-Aids come in now. Earle had no way of knowing how many companies would also think his idea was great and make their own brand of adhesive bandages. But he did know that his little idea made a big difference in people's lives.

The Band-Aid celebrates its one hundredth anniversary in 2020, and in spite of all the global competition today, Band-Aid brand adhesive bandages are still the boo-boo king.

EARLE DICKSON TIME LINE

1892 Earle Ensign Dickson is born in Grandview, Tennessee, on October 10, 1892.

1913 Earle graduates from Yale University, in Connecticut.

1916 Earle is hired as a cotton buyer for the Chicopee Manufacturing Company in Massachusetts, a subsidiary of Johnson & Johnson (J & J). Soon thereafter he moves to New Brunswick, New Jersey, to work for the parent company as a cotton buyer.

WWI Earle serves on special duty with the War Department during World War I.

1917 Earle marries Josephine Frances Knight.

1920 Earle devises a simple sterile dressing that Josephine can apply to her own hand or arm.

The first Band-Aids are handmade and marketed by J & J.

1924 Band-Aids are first mass-produced.

1925 Earle officially files a "Surgical Dressing" patent (US 1612267 A).

Earle is promoted to Hospital Sales Division manager of J & J.

1927 Earle is made chairman of the Standardization Committee on Surgical Gauze and Adhesive products at J & J.

Earle is appointed president of the Middlesex General Hospital (now Robert Wood Johnson University Hospital) in New Brunswick, New Jersey.

1929 Earle is elected to J & J's board of directors.

1931 Earle is promoted to assistant vice president of J & J.

1932 Earle is promoted again, this time to vice president.

1950 *Doctor Dan the Bandage Man*, a Little Golden Book about a boy who needs a Band-Aid, is published. The book originally came with six Band-Aids. It is still in print today.

1957 Earle retires at the age of 64.

1961 Earle dies on September 21 at age 68.

1963 Band-Aids go into space for the first time with NASA's Mercury astronauts.

1969 Josephine Knight Dickson dies at age 72. Josephine and Earle are buried together in New Brunswick, New Jersey.

2017 Earle is inducted posthumously into the National Inventors Hall of Fame.

OTHER MEDICAL INVENTIONS FROM THE 1920s AND 1930s

What Can You Find Out About How These Came to Be?

Note that there is much dispute about many of these dates. Sometimes the date indicates when the first use happened; other times, when the discovery or invention was patented. Sometimes it reflects when the invention was first used successfully in a lab (often on an animal); other times, when humans were the patients for the first time. All the dates below are approximate.

1921 Insulin discovered, first used to treat diabetes.

First vaccine for tuberculosis.

1922 Vitamin E first isolated and properties discovered.

1923 Cotton swabs invented.

First vaccine for diphtheria.

1924 First vaccine for tetanus.

1925 First vaccine for pertussis, or whooping cough.

1928 Iron lung first used.

1929 Penicillin introduced.

1932 Opaque dye injections used.

DeBakey roller pump invented, later used for open-heart surgery.

1937 First vaccine for yellow fever.

First vaccine for typhus.

First blood bank established in the United States.

LEARN MORE

One of the best ways to get more information is to type search terms into your favorite search engine. You can search for "history of the Band-Aid," "biography of Earle Dickson," and more. On YouTube, search for "Band-Aid commercial" with any decade or year to find vintage commercials. The music for the famous jingle "I Am Stuck on Band-Aid" was written by Barry Manilow.

Band-Aid Brand Time Line
A useful history of the Band-Aid.
http://www.band-aid.com/brand-heritage/history-info

Band-Aids: Still Sticking Around
News report about the history of the Band-Aid.
http://www.cbsnews.com/videos/band-aids-still-sticking-around/

How to Use a Band-Aid Brand Adhesive Bandage
History of traveling salesmen and early Band-Aids.
http://www.kilmerhouse.com/2008/09/how-to-use-a-band-aid-brand-adhesive-bandage/

Seventy-Five Years of Band-Aid
Includes photos of old Band-Aid boxes and one of Josephine.
http://www.savetz.com/bandaid/

This One's for the Wounded
Explains what we did before Band-Aids when we got hurt.
http://tedium.co/2015/05/19/history-of-bandages/

The Truly Bloody History: A Band-Aid Love Story
History of the Band-Aid in a fun video.
https://www.youtube.com/watch?v=b7VA5L9KH20